IMAGINE THAT!

POEMS OF NEVER-WAS

SELECTED BY **JACK PRELUTSKY**
ILLUSTRATED BY **KEVIN HAWKES**

ALFRED A. KNOPF

New York

In memory of Margrit Weiss
—J. P.

to Philly
—K. H.

Permissions acknowledgments for previously published material can be found on page 44.

www.randomhouse.com/kids/

Printed in the United States of America

Library of Congress Cataloging-in-Publication Data
Imagine that! : poems of never-was / selected by Jack Prelutsky ; illustrated by Kevin Hawkes.
p. cm.
Summary: An illustrated collection of poems about imaginary things, by such authors as
Jane Yolen, Conrad Aiken, and Karla Kuskin.
1. Imagination—Juvenile poetry. 2. Children's poetry, American. [1. Imagination—Poetry.
2. American poetry—Collections.]
I. Prelutsky, Jack. II. Hawkes, Kevin, ill.
PS595.I46I43 1998
811.008'09282—dc21
96-45591

ISBN 0-679-88206-5 (trade)
ISBN 0-679-98206-X (lib. bdg.)

10 9 8 7 6 5 4 3 2 1
First Edition

Old Cans

Old cans, boxes, wire
And any old junk
    is good
  If you want to make
    some sculpture.
You can make a cow
    . . . or a horse
  or maybe even a vulture.
You can stick
    them together
or tie them
    with some string,
And if it doesn't
    Look like a real animal
At least it will look
    like SOMETHING.

            —*Arnold Spilka*

Wind Pictures

Look! There's a giant stretching in the sky,
A thousand white-maned horses flying by,
A house, a mother mountain with her hills,
A lazy lady posing in her frills,
Cotton floating from a thousand bales,
And a white ship with white sails.

See the old witch fumbling with her shawl,
White towers piling on a castle wall,
The bits of soft that break and fall away,
Airborne mushrooms with undersides of gray—
Above, a white doe races with her fawn
On the white grass of a celestial lawn.
Lift up your lovely heads and look
As wind turns clouds into a picture book.

—*Mary O'Neill*

My Creature

I made a creature
out of clay,
just what it is
is hard to say.
Its neck is thin,
its legs are fat,
it's like a bear
and like a bat.

It's like a snake
and like a snail,
it has a little
curly tail,
a shaggy mane,
a droopy beard,
its ears are long,
its smile is weird.

It has four horns,
one beady eye,
two floppy wings
(though it can't fly),
it only sits
upon my shelf—
just think, I made it
by myself!

—Jack Prelutsky

The Paint Box

"Cobalt and umber and ultramarine,
   Ivory black and emerald green—
   What shall I paint to give pleasure to you?"
"Paint for me somebody utterly new."

"I have painted you tigers in crimson and white."
"The colors were good and you painted aright."
"I have painted the cook and a camel in blue
   And a panther in purple." "You painted them true.

"Now mix me a color that nobody knows,
   And paint me a country where nobody goes.
   And put in it people a little like you,
   Watching a unicorn drinking the dew."

—E. V. Rieu

U.F.O.

Hear that humming…
Spaceship's coming.

Watch that light…
It's shining bright.

Feel that air…
It's landing there.

Hear that roar…
Look at the door.

See the crew…
They're coming through!

—*Barbara Ireson*

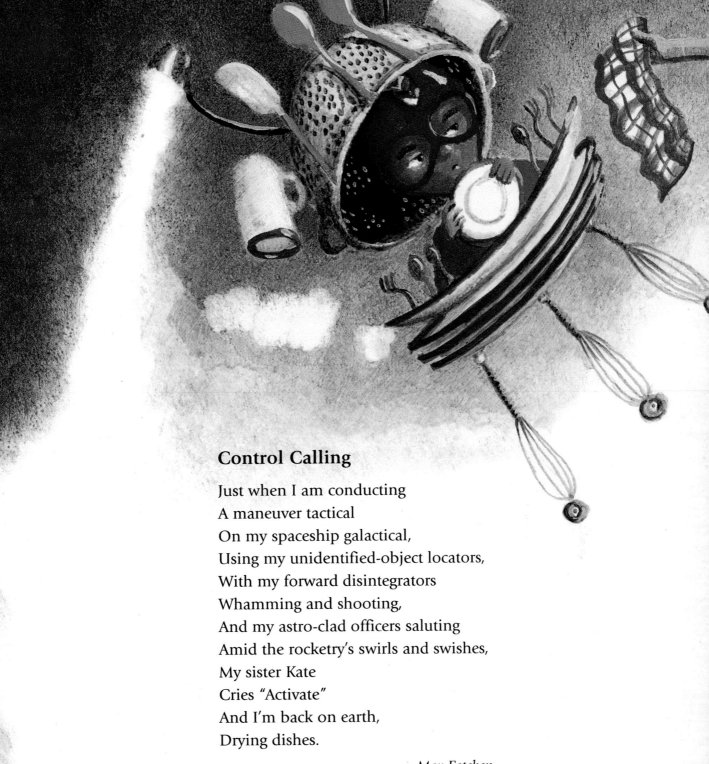

Control Calling

Just when I am conducting
A maneuver tactical
On my spaceship galactical,
Using my unidentified-object locators,
With my forward disintegrators
Whamming and shooting,
And my astro-clad officers saluting
Amid the rocketry's swirls and swishes,
My sister Kate
Cries "Activate"
And I'm back on earth,
Drying dishes.

—*Max Fatchen*

The Leathery Gumberoo

A beast that lives till it explodes
   Is the Leathery Gumberoo.
A foolish man once photographed one,
   But the picture blew up, too.

             —*Ennis Rees*

The Nonny

The Nonny-bird I love particularly;
   All day she chirps her joysome odes.
She rises perpendicularly,
   And if she goes too far, explodes.

            —*James Reeves*

12

The Thing Extraordinaire!

Oh, you should have been there
Listening to the whizz
Of curtains opening and the sudden blare
Of someone's voice announcing:
"Kiddies, here he is
Half man, half beast—The Thing Extraordinaire!"

Oh, you should have been there,
Oh, you should have seen
His tusks, his plume, his fur, his twisted hat,
The way when, walking upright,
He always seemed to lean,
His shadow slinking round him like a cat.

Oh, you should have been there,
Oh, you should have heard
The gruff and ghostly grunting from his snout,
His burble like a geyser,
His whistle like a bird,
The swish-swosh as he waved his tail about.

Oh, you should have been there,
Oh, you should have known
The thrill that filled us when we watched him dance:
His arms flung up like antlers,
His feet clumped down like stone,
His silver eyelids flickering in a trance;

Then he sort of shimmered
And seemed to fade away,
He faded…but that's not quite what I mean…
Exactly how he vanished
I'm not prepared to say—
You should have been there, oh, you should have been!

—*Richard Edwards*

The Alphabet Monster

I'm the Alphabet Monster
And nothing tastes better
To the Alphabet Monster
Than eating a letter.
A "j" and an "a"
And a "c" and a "k"
And the million more letters
I munch every day.

I'm hungry now.
What shall I do?
I think I'll eat
a "y"
an "o"
and a "u."

That means…YOU!

—Robert Heidbreder

The Flunnel

I've a letter called FLUNN. And the FLUNN is for Flunnel,
A softish nice fellow who hides in a tunnel.
He *only* comes out of his hole, I'm afraid,
When the right kind of softish nice music is played
On a kind of a hunting horn called the o'Grunth.
And to learn how to play it takes month after month
Of practicing, practicing. Isn't much fun-th.
And besides, it's quite heavy. Weighs almost a tun-th.
That's why few people bother to play the o'Grunth
So the Flunnel's been out of his tunnel just one-th.

—Dr. Seuss

The Flotz

I am the Flotz, I gobble dots,
indeed, I gobble lots and lots,
every dot I ever see
is bound to be a bite for me.
I often munch on myriads
of sweet, abundant periods,
I nibble hyphens, and with ease
chew succulent apostrophes.

From time to time, I turn my gaze
to little dotted "i's" and "j's,"
and if I chance upon a dash,
I soon dispatch it with panache.
I chomp on commas half the day,
quotation marks are rarer prey,
a semicolon's quite a treat,
while polka dots are joys to eat.

When I confront a dotted line,
my tongue flicks out, those dots are mine,
Morse code becomes a feast, and yes,
I've snacked upon an S.O.S.
For I'm the Flotz, who gobbles dots,
I gobble them in pails and pots,
and you'll not like my brief embrace
if you have freckles on your face.

—*Jack Prelutsky*

Mr. Mad's Machine

Mr. Mad has made a machine
To take you round the world.
Its wheels are square. Its tail is long.
Its wings are thin and curled.

It blows out rings of purple smoke.
The engine squeaks and squeals.
The jets are very powerful.
They're made of cotton reels.

I wonder what it would be like
To fly in this machine.
It is the strangest sort of plane
That I have ever seen!

—Tony Mitton

The Hum Bug Machine

The Hum Bug Machine
    teaches big bugs to hum,
As they sit on the Hum Bug's
    mechanical thumb.
This machine's very grumpy
    and has been for years,
For it can't stand the big bugs
    that hum in its gears.
"Hum Bug!" it grumbles,
    while stamping its feet,
"I'd rather make bugs
    into humbugger meat."

—Donna Lugg Pape

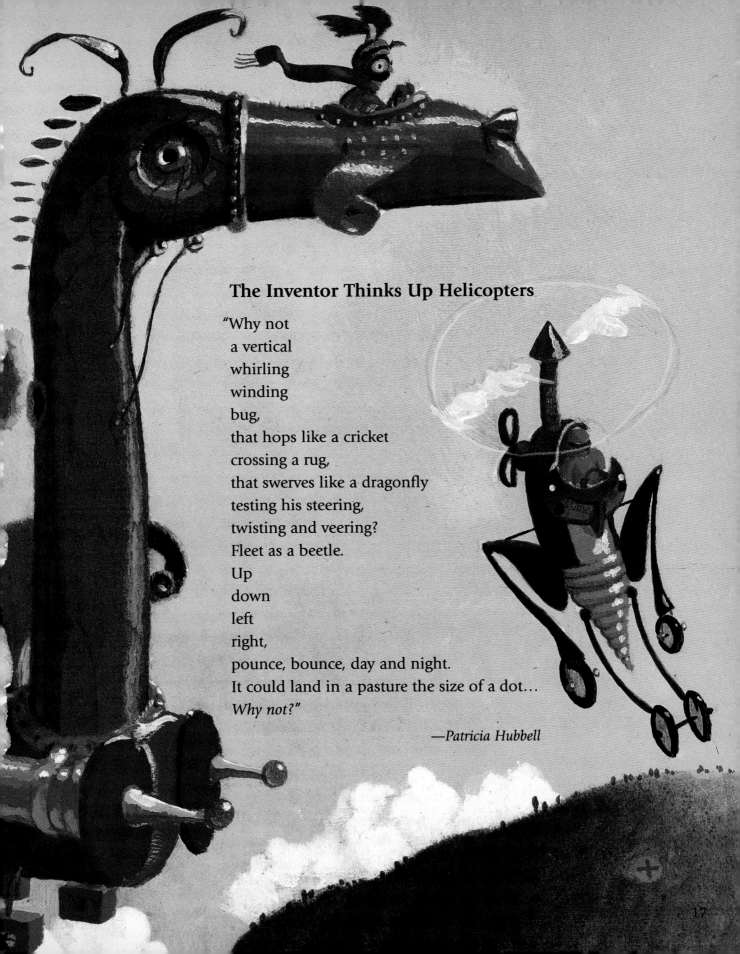

The Inventor Thinks Up Helicopters

"Why not
a vertical
whirling
winding
bug,
that hops like a cricket
crossing a rug,
that swerves like a dragonfly
testing his steering,
twisting and veering?
Fleet as a beetle.
Up
down
left
right,
pounce, bounce, day and night.
It could land in a pasture the size of a dot…
Why not?"

—Patricia Hubbell

The Subbergump

The Subbergump is not a whale,
Nor a fish, though he swims in the ocean.
He's a sort of submarine garbage pail,
Who dines in perpetual motion
By following ships from land to land
And swallowing tidbits secondhand.

He breakfasts on bones and orange peels
That the cook has thrown in the sea.
Last week's meat loaf makes midday meals,
And he often has soapsuds for tea.

And yet, in his heart, he dares to hope
For a super Subbergump feast.
Keeping constant watch with his periscope,
He's a hungry but patient beast!

So when you go on an ocean ship,
Don't forget that he loves lemon custard.
You can sneak him bags of potato chips
And dozens of hot dogs with mustard.
Delighted, he'll grin as he makes his swim
Toward food that was specially meant for HIM!

—*Carol Newman*

The Crim

The Crim cries a river
Of tears as it weeps.
It bawls by the barrel
And sobs as it sleeps.
It often looks gloomy
And always looks grim.
It's certainly lucky
It knows how to swim.

—*Douglas Florian*

The Giraft

If you're out in the ocean, afloat on the deep,
With the sharks making straight for your craft,
Simply close your eyes tightly and whistle a shrill
S.O.S. for the nearest Giraft.

If you plan to be going away on a cruise
And you find your lifeboats understaffed,
Do not give it a thought, simply whistle a tune
That will call on the nearest Giraft.

For they sail very swiftly, can outpace a sub,
And their periscope necks fore and aft
Let them keep a sharp eye on the ocean so no
One can sneak up behind a Giraft.

I have rowed many miles and have sailed quite a few,
And on none of those trips have I laughed,
For my travels all filled me with fear and with dread
Till I learned of the friendly Giraft.

—*Jane Yolen*

19

The Ogglewop

The Ogglewop is tall and wide,
And though he looks quite passive,
He's crammed with boys and girls inside,
—That's why he is so massive!

—*Colin West*

Monster Mothers

When monster mothers get together
they brag about their babies.
The other day I heard one say,
"He got his very first fang today!"

"Mine is ugly."
"Mine is mean."
"Mine is turning
  nice and green."

"Mine's as scaly
  as a fish."
"Mine is sort of
  yellowish."

"Mine breathes fire
  and smoke and such."
"Mine has skin
  you'd hate to touch."

"Mine smells like
an old sardine."
"Mine's the weirdest
thing you've seen."

"Mine has strong and
ugly jaws."
"Mine has sharp and
dreadful claws."

"Mine has two heads."
"Mine has four!"
"Mine is learning
how to roar."

When monster mothers get together
they brag about their babies.
The other day I heard one say,
"He ate his very first kid today!"

—Florence Parry Heide

21

The Splinter Cat

The Splinter Cat, in search of fun,
    Dives from tree to tree,
And everyone it dives upon
    Is splintered totally.

—*Ennis Rees*

The Crocodial

The dime goes in the Crocodial,
Crocodial, Crocodial,
It only takes a little while
Until your call goes through.

He chews the dime in little bits,
Little bits, little bits,
And then disgorges all the pits.
That's when your call goes through.

Don't be upset by his broad smile,
His broad smile, his broad smile,
He's a *dime*-atarian Crocodial,
Until your call goes through.

—*Jane Yolen*

22

Bobcaterpillar

Bobcaterpillar's umpteen feet
  are always spick and span and neat,
he sits and washes all day long,
  and sings his little washing-song.
"Wash your eyebrows, wash your lashes,
  wash your BYOOOTIFUL moustaches,
wash each ear, and then, my dear,
  carefully wash BEHIND that ear.
Am I head? Or am I tail—?
  Wash it all. And NEVER fail
to scrub each toe-and-finger-nail!"
  See him winding all about
almost turning inside out
  just to get AT those umpteen feet,
AND those hands, to keep them neat!
  Now he props his looking-glass
up against a blade of grass
  or a purple head of clover
there to look himself all over.
  "Am I spick? And am I span?
Preened and polished ALL I can?"
  And he's pleased, and purrs, and lifts
a teeny comb, and with it sifts
  one by one those lovely lashes
and those BYOOOTIFUL moustaches:
  combs each pointed little ear,
coils around to comb his rear,
  and—he's finished!—Well, what then?
Why, he'll wash it all again.

                —*Conrad Aiken*

23

I Have a Secret Dragon

I have a secret dragon
Who is living in the tub,
It greets me when I take a bath,
And gives my back a scrub.
My parents cannot see it,
They don't suspect it's there,
They look in its direction,
And all they see is air.

My dragon's very gentle,
My dragon's very kind,
No matter how I pull its tail,
My dragon doesn't mind.
We splash around together
And play at silly things,
Then when I'm finished bathing,
It dries me with its wings.

—*Jack Prelutsky*

24

The Gold-Tinted Dragon

What's the good of a wagon
Without any dragon
To pull you for mile after mile?
An elegant lean one
A gold-tinted green one
Wearing a dragonly smile.
You'll sweep down the valleys
You'll sail up the hills
Your dragon will shine in the sun
And as you rush by
The people will cry
"I wish that my wagon had one!"

—*Karla Kuskin*

25

Onkerpled

If a Glomp is hiding
Beneath your bed,
Don't be afraid—
Yell "onkerpled."

Glomps may be scary
And their whiskers are red,
But they run away quickly
If you yell "onkerpled"

LOUDLY.

—*Michael Dugan*

The Snoffle

I'm not afraid of monsters
or any witch or bat.
I'm not afraid of skeletons
or anything like that.
I'm not afraid of tigers
or a big, man-eating shark.
I'm not afraid of giants
and I really like the dark.

BUT

I *am* afraid of Snoffles—
They really frighten me.
A Snoffle is an awful thing,
a ghastly sight to see.
So if I see a Snoffle
I know just what I'll do.
I'll put it in a great big box
and send it off to you!

—*Florence Parry Heide*

26

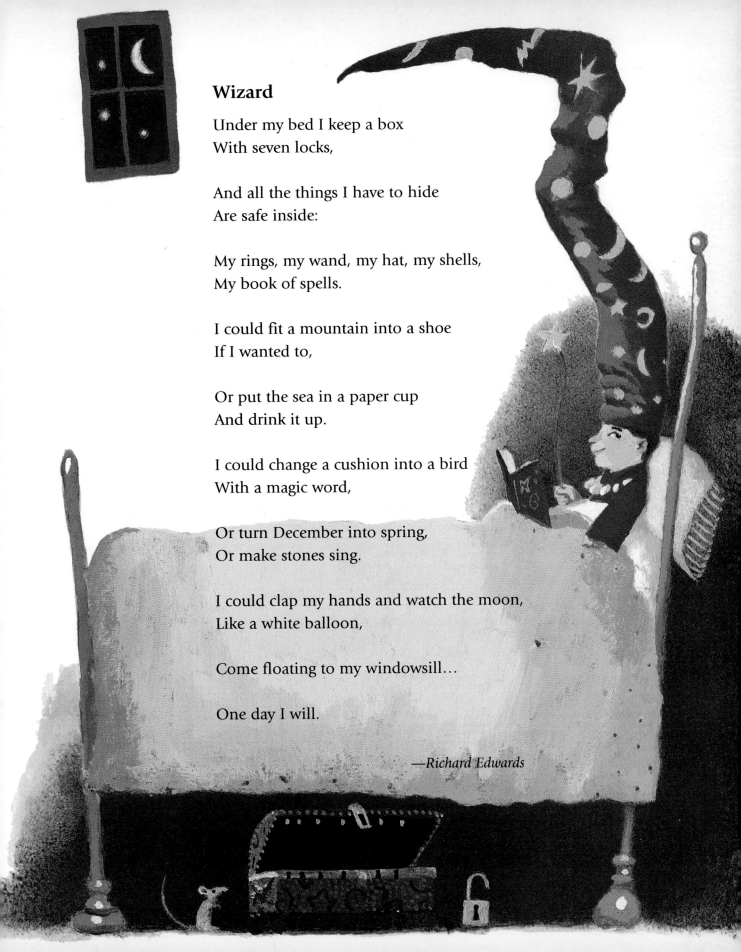

Wizard

Under my bed I keep a box
With seven locks,

And all the things I have to hide
Are safe inside:

My rings, my wand, my hat, my shells,
My book of spells.

I could fit a mountain into a shoe
If I wanted to,

Or put the sea in a paper cup
And drink it up.

I could change a cushion into a bird
With a magic word,

Or turn December into spring,
Or make stones sing.

I could clap my hands and watch the moon,
Like a white balloon,

Come floating to my windowsill...

One day I will.

—Richard Edwards

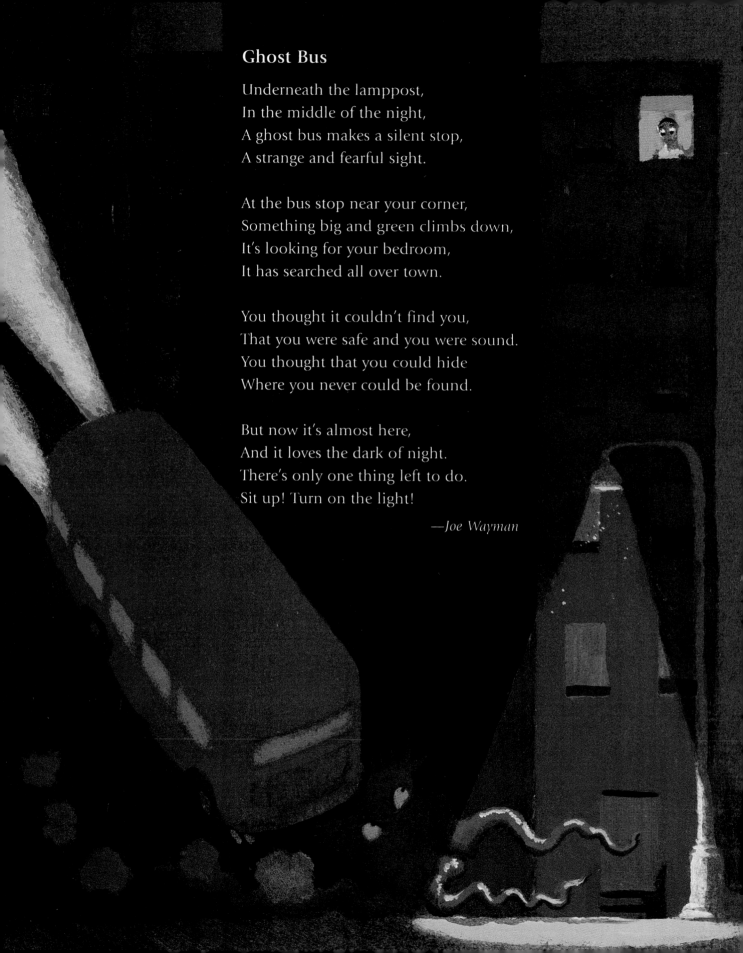

Ghost Bus

Underneath the lamppost,
In the middle of the night,
A ghost bus makes a silent stop,
A strange and fearful sight.

At the bus stop near your corner,
Something big and green climbs down,
It's looking for your bedroom,
It has searched all over town.

You thought it couldn't find you,
That you were safe and you were sound.
You thought that you could hide
Where you never could be found.

But now it's almost here,
And it loves the dark of night.
There's only one thing left to do.
Sit up! Turn on the light!

—Joe Wayman

The Gottle

Thin as a new moon, if not as bright,
the leathery Gottle comes out at night

and, thinking hard,
tiptoes and hops around the yard

and, thinking the stars are flies,
tries

to catch a few for dinner.
And gets thinner & thinner.

—Robert Wallace

The Blomp

They say that when the sun goes down,
That's when the Blomp walks into town,
And it whistles till the break of day.
Anyway, that's what they say.
I've heard that when the skies are dark
The Blomp strolls gaily through the park,
And whistles tunes just like a bird.
Anyway, that's what I've heard.
Now, if some black and spooky night
You step outside to see this sight,
The Blomp will eat your shoes and hat.
Nobody ever tells you that.

—Harvey Rudoff

The Phillyloo Bird

The Phillyloo Bird looks like a crane
   But has even longer legs.
Since it has no knees, it can't sit down,
   So it lays only broken eggs.

               —Ennis Rees

Ookpik

An Ookpik is nothing but hair.
If you shave him, he isn't there.

He's never locked in the zoo.
He lives in a warm igloo.

He can whistle and dance on the walls.
He can dance on Niagara Falls.

He has nothing at all on his mind.
If you scratch him, he wags his behind.

He dances from morning to night.
Then he blinks. That turns out the light.

               —Dennis Lee

The Wendigo

The Wendigo,
The Wendigo!
Its eyes are ice and indigo!
Its blood is rank and yellowish!
Its voice is hoarse and bellowish!
Its tentacles are slithery,
And scummy,
Slimy,
Leathery!
Its lips are hungry blubbery,
And smacky,
Sucky,
Rubbery!

The Wendigo,
The Wendigo!
I saw it just a friend ago!
Last night it lurked in Canada;
Tonight, on your veranada!
As you are lolling hammockwise
It contemplates you stomachwise.
You loll,
It contemplates,
It lollops.
The rest is merely gulps and gollops.

—*Ogden Nash*

The Finisher-Upper

To demolish a dinner
Or diminish a supper,
Why don't you call for
The Finisher-Upper?

Watch him demolish
And watch him diminish
Any old leftover food
He can finish.

His performance is always
So perfect and polished:
Suppers diminished
And dinners demolished!

—*Colin West*

Before You Fix Your Next
Peanut Butter Sandwich—Read This:

Globb's a tiny creature who
climbs into jars and waits for you.
Yes, that is where he's often hid.
He waits till you unscrew the lid,
then he leaps out—surprise, surprise!—
and grows to an enormous size.
Then do watch out, for in a minute
he'll grab the jar and stuff you in it
and there you'll sit, alas, alack,
until *he* wants a little snack.

—*Florence Parry Heide*

The Spangled Pandemonium

The Spangled Pandemonium
Is missing from the zoo.
He bent the bars the barest bit,
And slithered glibly through.

He crawled across the moated wall,
He climbed the mango tree,
And when his keeper scrambled up,
He nipped him in the knee.

To all of you, a warning
Not to wander after dark,
Or if you must, make very sure
You stay out of the park.

For the Spangled Pandemonium
Is missing from the zoo,
And since he nipped his keeper,
He would just as soon nip you!

—*Palmer Brown*

Multikertwigo

I saw the Multikertwigo
Standing on his head,
He was looking at me sideways
And this is what he said:
"Sniddle Iddle Ickle Thwack
Nicki-Nacki-Noo,
Biddle-diddle Dicky-Dack
Tickle-tockle-too!"
None of this made sense to me,
Maybe it does to you.

—*Spike Milligan*

The Quinquaped Jikes

The five-footed Jikes
Should be splendid on hikes
With his overabundance of toes.
But the silly old chap
Prefers taking a nap,
And if walking, he strolls on his nose.

—*Peter Wesley-Smith*

34

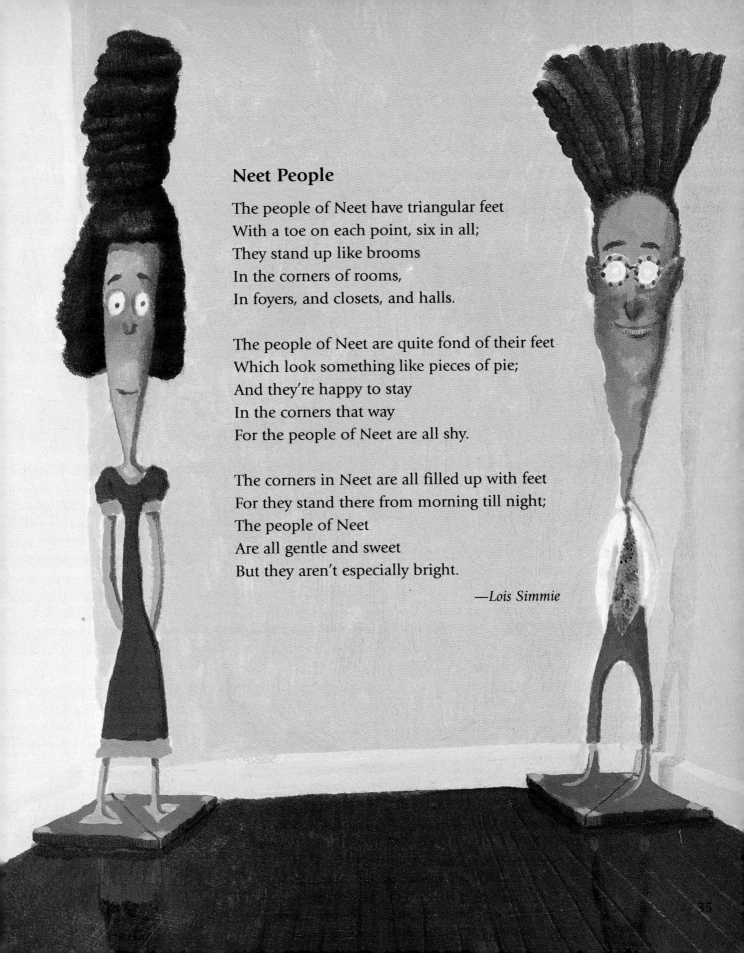

Neet People

The people of Neet have triangular feet
With a toe on each point, six in all;
They stand up like brooms
In the corners of rooms,
In foyers, and closets, and halls.

The people of Neet are quite fond of their feet
Which look something like pieces of pie;
And they're happy to stay
In the corners that way
For the people of Neet are all shy.

The corners in Neet are all filled up with feet
For they stand there from morning till night;
The people of Neet
Are all gentle and sweet
But they aren't especially bright.

—*Lois Simmie*

35

The Hairy-Nosed
Preposterous

The Hairy-Nosed Preposterous
Looks much like a Rhinosterous,
But also something like a tank—
For which he has himself to thank.

His ears are the size of tennis shoes,
His eyes the size of pins.
And when he lies down for a snooze
An orchestra begins.

It whistles, rattles, roars, and thumps,
And the wind of it comes and goes
Through the storm-tossed hair that grows in clumps
On the end of his capable nose.

—*John Ciardi*

The Drum-Tummied Snumm

From a country called Frumm
Comes this Drum-Tummied Snumm
Who can drum any tune
That you might care to hum.
(Doesn't hurt him a bit
'Cause his Drum-Tummy's numb.)

—*Dr. Seuss*

The Bugle-Billed Bazoo

The noisiest bird that ever grew
Is the Bugle-Billed Bazoo.
(He's even noisier than YOU.)

He starts his YAMMERING as soon
As he's awake, then SHOUTS till noon.

Then SCREAMS from noon till six or so,
And then he YELLS an hour or two.

He's not like other birds who sing
Because the flowers are out for Spring.

He SHRIEKS and SCOLDS the whole day through
Just to be heard. If you do, too,
YOU'RE a Bugle-Billed Bazoo.

—*John Ciardi*

37

The Land of the Bumbley Boo

In the Land of the Bumbley Boo
The people are red white and blue,
They never blow noses,
Or ever wear closes,
What a sensible thing to do!

In the Land of the Bumbley Boo
You can buy Lemon pie at the Zoo;
They give away Foxes
In little Pink Boxes
And Bottles of Dandylion Stew.

In the Land of the Bumbley Boo
You never see a Gnu,
But thousands of cats
Wearing trousers and hats
Made of Pumpkins and Pelican Glue!

CHORUS: Oh, the Bumbley Boo! the Bumbley Boo!
        That's the place for me and you!
        So hurry! Let's run!
        The train leaves at one!
        For the Land of the Bumbley Boo!
        The wonderful Bumbley Boo-Boo-Boo!
        The wonderful Bumbley BOO!!!

                              —*Spike Milligan*

Jabberwocky

'Twas brillig, and the slithy toves
   Did gyre and gimble in the wabe;
All mimsy were the borogoves,
   And the mome raths outgrabe.

"Beware the Jabberwock, my son!
   The jaws that bite, the claws that catch!
Beware the Jubjub bird, and shun
   The frumious Bandersnatch!"

He took his vorpal sword in hand;
   Long time the manxome foe he sought—
So rested he by the Tumtum tree,
   And stood awhile in thought.

And as in uffish thought he stood,
   The Jabberwock, with eyes of flame,
Came whiffling through the tulgey wood,
   And burbled as it came!

One, two! One, two! And through and through
   The vorpal blade went snicker-snack!
He left it dead, and with its head
   He went galumphing back.

"And hast thou slain the Jabberwock?
   Come to my arms, my beamish boy!
O frabjous day! Callooh! Callay!"
   He chortled in his joy.

'Twas brillig, and the slithy toves
   Did gyre and gimble in the wabe;
All mimsy were the borogoves,
   And the mome raths outgrabe.

—Lewis Carroll

39

Johnny Drew a Monster

Johnny drew a monster.
The monster chased him.
Just in time
Johnny erased him.

—*Lilian Moore*

Art

Down in the dumpster
The *artist* sees—
In spools of wire
And hooks and keys
In pipes and springs
And iron pans
In curtain rods
And rusted cans—
A sculpture
Suited
For a park.
Down in the dumpster
Deep and dark.

—*Eileen Spinelli*

I Never Saw

I never saw
          a ghost on stilts
a witch wrapped up
          in patchwork quilts
a dragon
in a wagon
or a wizard wearing kilts.

I said
I never *did*.
I didn't say
I never *may*.

—*Lilian Moore*

They Never Send Sam to the Store Anymore

The day they sent Sam to the grocery store
to purchase a carton of eggs,
he brought back a pear with a pearl in its core,
and a leopard with lavender legs.

He returned with an elephant small as a mouse,
a baseball that bounces a mile,
a little tame dragon that heats up the house,
and a lantern that lights when they smile.

Sam brought them a snowball that never feels cold,
a gossamer carpet that flies,
a salmon of silver, a grackle of gold,
and an ermine with emerald eyes.

They never send Sam to the store anymore,
no matter how often he begs,
for he brought back a dodo that danced on the floor,
but he didn't bring home any eggs.

—Jack Prelutsky

Ladder to the Sky

Do you know
If you try
You really can
Touch the sky?

Lean a ladder
Against the moon
And climb, climb high
Talk to the stars
And leave your handprints
All across the sky

Jump on a cloud
And spend the day
Trampoline-jumping
Through the air
Climb a rainbow
And watch the world
From way up there

Then ride that rainbow slide
Back home.

—*Sheree Fitch*

INDEX OF TITLES

INDEX OF AUTHORS

ACKNOWLEDGMENTS

Grateful acknowledgment is made to the following for permission to reprint previously published material:

Bantam Doubleday Dell Publishing Group, Inc., for "The Wizard" from *The Word Party* by Richard Edwards and John Lawrence, illustrator. Copyright © 1986 by Richard Edwards. Canadian rights are administered by James Clarke & Co. Ltd., The Lutterworth Press. Reprinted by permission of Delacorte Press, a division of Bantam Doubleday Dell Publishing Group, Inc., and James Clarke & Co. Ltd., The Lutterworth Press. "The Thing Extraordinaire!" from *A Mouse in My Roof* by Richard Edwards. Copyright © 1988 by Richard Edwards. Canadian rights are administered by Richard Edwards. Reprinted by permission of Delacorte Press, a division of Bantam Doubleday Dell Publishing Group, Inc., and Felicity Bryan Literary Agency for the author.

Boyds Mills Press for "The Bugle-Billed Bazoo" from *The Reason for the Pelican*. Copyright © 1994 by the family of John Ciardi. "The Hairy-Nosed Preposterous" from *Someone Could Win a Polar Bear*. Copyright © 1970 by John Ciardi. "Art" from *Where Is the Night Train Going?* Copyright © 1996 by Eileen Spinelli. All poems reprinted by permission of Boyds Mills Press. "Ladder to the Sky" from *Toes in My Nose*. Copyright © 1987 by Sheree Fitch. Canadian rights administered by Doubleday Canada Limited. Reprinted by permission of Boyds Mills Press and Doubleday Canada Limited.

Curtis Brown, Ltd., for "The Crocodial" from *How Beastly* published by Wordsong/Boyds Mills Press. Copyright © 1980 by Jane Yolen. Reprinted by permission of Curtis Brown, Ltd.

Laura Cecil Literary Agency for "The Nonny" from *Complete Poems for Children* published by Heinemann. Copyright © James Reeves. Reprinted by permission of the James Reeves Estate.

Michael Dugan for "Onkerpled" from *Stuff and Nonsense*. Copyright © 1977 by Michael Dugan. Reprinted by permission of the author.

Harcourt Brace & Company for "The Crim" from *Monster Motel*. Copyright © 1993 by Douglas Florian. "The Giraft" from *Animal Fare*. Copyright © 1994 by Jane Yolen. All poems reprinted by permission of Harcourt Brace & Company.

HarperCollins Publishers for "The Gold-Tinted Dragon" from *Dogs & Dragons, Trees & Dreams* by Karla Kuskin. Copyright © 1980 by Karla Kuskin. "The Spangled Pandemonium" from *Beyond the Paw Paw Trees* by Palmer Brown. Copyright © 1954 by Palmer Brown. All poems reprinted by permission of HarperCollins Publishers.

HarperCollins Publishers Australia for "The Quinquaped Jikes" from *The Ombley-Gombley* by Peter Wesley-Smith. Reprinted by permission of HarperCollins Publishers Australia.

Barbara Ireson for "U.F.O." from *Spaceman Spaceman and Other Rhymes* (Transworld, 1980). Reprinted by permission of the author.

John Johnson (Author's Agent) Ltd. for "Control Calling" from *Wry Rhymes for Troublesome Times* (Kestrel Books, London). Copyright © 1983 by Max Fatchen. Reprinted by permission of John Johnson (Author's Agent) Ltd. for the author.

The Lerner Group for "The Blomp" by Harvey Rudoff from *The Practically Complete Guide to Almost Real Musical Instruments for Nearly Everyone* (Lerner Publications, 1964). Reprinted by permission of The Lerner Group.